The
Hoop of Peace

Kevin Locke performing the hoop dance.

THE

HOOP OF PEACE

Jan Havnen-Finley

Illustrated by
Ken "Rainbow Cougar" Edwards

Naturegraph Publishers

Library of Congress Cataloging-in-Publication Data

Havnen-Finley, Jan, 1949-   The hoop of peace: by Jan Havnen-
Finley; illustrated by Ken "Rainbow Cougar" Edwards.   p.   cm.
ISBN 0-87961-239-8 : $7.95 1. Dakota dance. 2. Hoop dance—
Great Plains. 3. Dakota Indians—Rites and ceremonies. 4. Dakota
Indians—Religion. I. Title.
E99.D1H35   1994
299'.74—dc20   94-29742   CIP

Photographs by Jan and Ryan Finley

Books for a better world
Naturegraph Publishers
P.O. Box 1075
Happy Camp, CA 96039

Dedicated to

Charles Locke and Arlo Good Bear

ACKNOWLEDGEMENTS

A warm and loving thank you to Patricia Locke who reviewed the initial manuscript, to Kevin Locke for sharing this story, and to all those whose individual assistance became a unified strength in putting this book together.

INTRODUCTION

The Hoop of Peace, by Jan Havnen-Finley, is written in a style suitable to young readers, but its message is important for all ages. It is a story of Kevin Locke, or *Tokaheya Inajin* ("Stands First" in Lakota), who leads us through his art of the Lakota hoop dance to understand the great vision of the Sioux holy man, Black Elk (1863 - 1950). When Black Elk was nine years old, and his people were still flourishing and living peacefully on the northern prairie, which was blessed with tall grasses and abundant buffalo, he was granted a great vision. He foresaw the withering of the sacred tree of his people and the stages of suffering through which they must pass before this tree would blossom once again. The tree, growing within the sacred hoop of the Lakota nation, represents the spirit of the people and everything good and holy. The hoop symbolizes not only the unity of the people, but the integration and unity of all living things in one balanced whole.

In 1890, Black Elk survived the massacre of Indians by U.S. soldiers at Wounded Knee near Pine Ridge, South Dakota. Some forty years later, he recalled with infinite sadness:

> I can still see the butchered women and children lying heaped and scattered all along the crooked gulch as plain as when I saw them with eyes still young. And I can see that something else died there in the bloody mud, and was buried in the blizzard. A people's dream died there. It was a beautiful dream.

Black Elk thought that he had failed to restore his people's hope. He prayed that part of the sacred tree would still live in their hearts and that they would return once more to the sacred hoop, the good red road, and the sheltering tree. In his great vision, Black Elk had been shown that this time would come. More significantly, however, not only had he seen his own people regain their spirit and mend their sacred hoop, but he had seen the hoop of the Lakota nation joined together with the hoops of many other nations, intertwined in one great circle, representing the hoop of all mankind. Within this world hoop, the sacred tree blossomed anew in multi-colored splendor.

The new sacred tree that Black Elk saw sheltering all people is the hope of the future. A new consciousness will be born in human hearts. People of one race or religion will no longer look down upon others of different races or religions. Instead, they will see each other as brothers and sisters, and will rejoice in the beauty of unity in diversity. Whatever is good and beautiful in every native tradition

7

all over the world, each nation's flowering tree and sacred hoop, will be preserved and shared as gifts with the rest of humankind.

Black Elk was not the only person to foresee the eventual unity of humankind in one sacred hoop. In the East, in the direction of the day-break star, One who was neither Indian nor Wasichu (the Lakota term for the Europeans), the Bahá'i prophet Bahá'u'lláh (1817 - 1892), came to heal the world with tidings that peace and security can only be attained through unity. "The earth is but one country and mankind its citizens." He taught that the essential principles of the world's great religions are in harmony.

Kevin Locke, a Lakota from the Standing Rock Reservation in South Dakota, is proof that the sacred tree of understanding is still blossoming. He was formerly an elementary school teacher and principal on the Standing Rock Reservation, where he still resides with his wife Dorothy and their daughters, Kimimila and Waniya, and their son, Ohiyesa. He gave up his teaching position to communicate Bahá'u'lláh's mission of a united world through the arts. He has performed for audiences on every continent of the globe in over sixty countries. Besides being a master hoop dancer, Locke has perfected the art of playing the Indian flute, recording *Dream Catcher* in 1992. He is also a storyteller, and narrated a cassette, *The Flood and Other Lakota Stories* (Parabola 1993). For his role in preserving traditional arts, Locke was awarded the National Heritage Fellowship, the highest national award in this category, by President George Bush in 1990.

Kevin Locke works for unity, and he uses the most uncontroversial of all mediums, art, to teach it. In his hoop performance, after demonstrating with his hoop designs such natural wonders as grass growing, a butterfly, a tree or an eagle, he ends by forming his twenty-eight black, red, yellow, and white hoops into a fragile ball. "The world is like that", he says. "It must be held together with love and understanding".

Although he uses Lakota lore in his presentations, Kevin Locke seeks to communicate across cultural lines. He explains:

> My presentation is all geared to perpetuate or to convey the positive awareness of the oneness of humankind. And I do that through culture-specific performances of traditional music and dance. My goal is...to penetrate to the core of these traditions and find those universal human values that are enshrined at the core of all cultures, all people.

8

Andrew Bacskai, a writer for the Minneapolis *Weekly Guide to Arts and Entertainment* notes:

> The theme of oneness inherent in Locke's material is central to his presentational style as well. In an effort to break down the barrier between performer and audience, Locke encourages audience members to dance and sing with him. His performances unfold more like celebrations than theatrical pieces.

Another art critic, Jeff Bartlett, Executive Director of the Minneapolis Southern Theater says:

> Kevin exudes more joy from the stage than any other performer I've seen....His is not music for the sake of entertainment; it is more like speaking from the heart—taking images from the heart and communicating them through music.

The Hoop of Peace will help inspire a new generation to follow in the footsteps of Kevin Locke. Each person has a boundless potential within herself or himself and a unique gift to give. May we each do our part to foster unity, fellowship, and understanding between the diverse cultures of humanity.

Keven Brown
January, 1994

9

A Story for All Ages

Even though many golden and crimson suns have risen

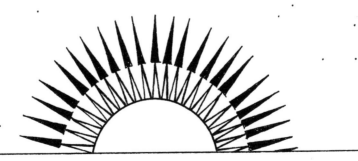

and set,

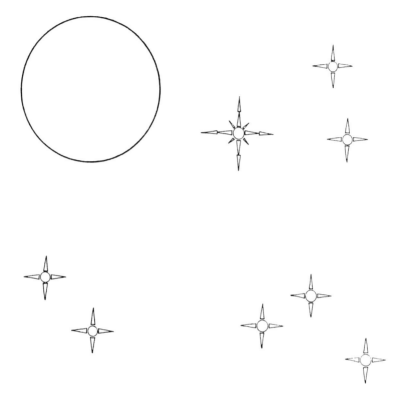

and even though many opalescent* moons have appeared in the nighttime heavens since the time of the first American Indian hoop dancer,

* opalescent (o-pa-les-sent)... a play of colors like an opal

the art lives on.

There are only a few hoop dancers left to enliven the flowing waters of present day time with this traditional art movement. Tokaheya Inajin* is one of the few.

*Tokaheya Inajin, (Tok-a-hey-a In-a-jin) — Kevin Locke's Lakota name; it means Stands First.

Tokaheya Inajin shares the hoop dance, a cultural gift from the American Indian people, with the rest of humanity.

Ever since he can remember, Tokaheya Inajin loved to watch hoop dancers. Their high-spirited dancing made him feel happy inside. He dreamed that someday he too might be given the honor of bringing smiles of happiness to his fellow people through dance.

His "someday" dream came true. One day, when Tokaheya Inajin was about twenty-four years old, his good friend, Arlo Good Bear, took the time to teach him a few basic hoop designs. It was a privilege for Tokaheya Inajin to receive this gift from his friend. Usually the movements of each hoop dancer's dance are kept a secret. That way others can't copy the patterns and destroy the uniqueness of each individual dance. It takes a lot of time to develop each artistic design.

A short time after he had taught Tokaheya Inajin a few of the basic hoop patterns, Arlo Good Bear died. Arlo was only twenty-one years old. Tokaheya Inajin missed his dear friend who had passed on to the world beyond this one.

After Arlo Good Bear's body was returned to Mother Earth, Arlo came to Tokaheya Inajin in a dream. In his dream, Arlo Good Bear looked down on him, smiled, and then soared off into the heavens. After this dream, Tokaheya Inajin began to dream of hoops. Many beautiful designs came to him in his sleep. When he awoke, he would form these harmonious circular patterns with his hoops so that he would remember them.

This was the beginning of what Tokaheya Inajin now shares with people all over the world. Each circular pattern represents a level of creation.

His hoop designs give people a chance to use their imaginations.

The imagination can see such things as:

The sun and the moon,

grass sprouting,

a flower,

a butterfly,

and even an eagle.

The eagle is very special to Tokaheya Inajin. It represents such noble attributes as grandeur and loftiness. The eagle reminds him that our thoughts need to rise as high as the eagles soar — way, way up to the rarified atmosphere where the air is pure and fresh.

The hoop itself is also very special to Tokaheya Inajin because of its circular shape. The circle describes many things — interconnectedness, unity, harmony. To the Lakota people, the circle symbolizes PEACE. Tokaheya Inajin belongs to the Lakota nation. From the Lakota nation came a very special man by the name of Black Elk. Black Elk was an Indian holy man who had visions of things to come. Tokaheya's Inajin's hoop dance reflects the fruition of Black Elk's vision of the future.*

This vision came to Black Elk at the age of nine. For more information regarding Black Elk's vision see *Black Elk Speaks* by John G. Neihardt (University of Nebraska Press, 1961).

Black Elk looked ahead to a time when he saw the American Indian people climbing upward on a very treacherous journey. He saw four levels in the journey of his vision. Each level of ascent represented a generation.

At the end of the first ascent, the people camped together in a circle and in the center of this sacred circle stood a holy tree.

By the time the people reached the end of the second ascent, they became troubled, restless, and afraid. The leaves began to fall from the holy tree.

The journey to the third level was filled with many difficulties. Each person followed his own vision, people ran in confusion and were no longer together. The whole universe carried the sound of war in the winds. By the time the people reached the highest point of the third ascent, the nation's hoop was broken. It was no longer a circle. The holy tree seemed to be dying.

When the people began the journey of the fourth ascent, the holy tree was gone and the people were starving. This is what Black Elk saw and it made him very sad, so sad that he began to weep. As he wept, he saw on the north side of the starving camp a sacred man painted red. The sacred man walked into the center, reclined, and then began to roll. As he rolled, a fat bison took his place. And where the bison stood, a sacred herb sprouted and blossomed — right in the center of the nation's hoop, in the very same spot where the tree had been. Four bright and beautiful blossoms — one black, one white, one red, and one yellow — formed on the herb's single stem. The brilliant rays of each blossom "flashed to the heavens".

41

Before long, the flowering tree was back again at the center of the nation's hoop — right where the four-rayed herb had blossomed. In his vision, Black Elk was then given the four-rayed herb to carry with him as the people took the final, most difficult steps of all — the steps toward the fourth ascent.

It was dark and terrible. The whole world was
screaming for the "winds of the world were fighting."
After a time the earth became covered in a blanket
of stillness. And out of this stillness a soft song
emerged which filled the entire world and rippled the
silence. It was so beautiful that the whole universe
began to dance — nothing could remain still. The
dark clouds passed over, blessing the people with
friendly rain and a flaming rainbow. This is when
Black Elk saw the hoop of the whole world.

It was a different hoop than the one that had broken. It was a hoop of many interconnected hoops that made one circle. It was as "wide as daylight and as starlight" and in the center of this hoop of many hoops grew one mighty flowering tree to shelter all of humanity.

It was a sacred hoop.

Tokaheya Inajin gives us a visual image of this sacred hoop of many hoops at the end of his dance. He uses the symbols of his artistic hoop designs to carry the universal message of hope for unity and peace to people all over the world.

The hoops show us that people of all colors are brothers and sisters under one Great Spirit. Together we can form **The Great Hoop Of Peace** by widening our circle of compassion to include the entire human species.

Nothing exists in isolation.